UPSIDE DOWN LIVING

violence

[
The Upside-Down Living series emphasizes living out
one's Christian faith through the lens of Jesus
by following values that seem so countercultural
they appear to be upside down.
]

J. Fred Kauffman

Herald Press

Harrisonburg, Virginia

Upside-Down Living
Violence

© 2017 by Herald Press, Harrisonburg, Virginia 22802. 800-245-7894.
All rights reserved.
International Standard Book Number: 978-1-5138-0171-1
Printed in United States of America

Written by J. Fred Kauffman
Design by Merrill Miller
Cover photo by Zoonar RF/Thinkstock (composite image)
Cartoons by Timothy Kauffman

Unless otherwise noted, Scripture text is quoted, with permission,
from the *New Revised Standard Version*, © 1989, Division of Christian
Education of the National Council of Churches of Christ in the United
States of America.

20 19 18 17   10 9 8 7 6 5 4 3 2 1

[Contents]

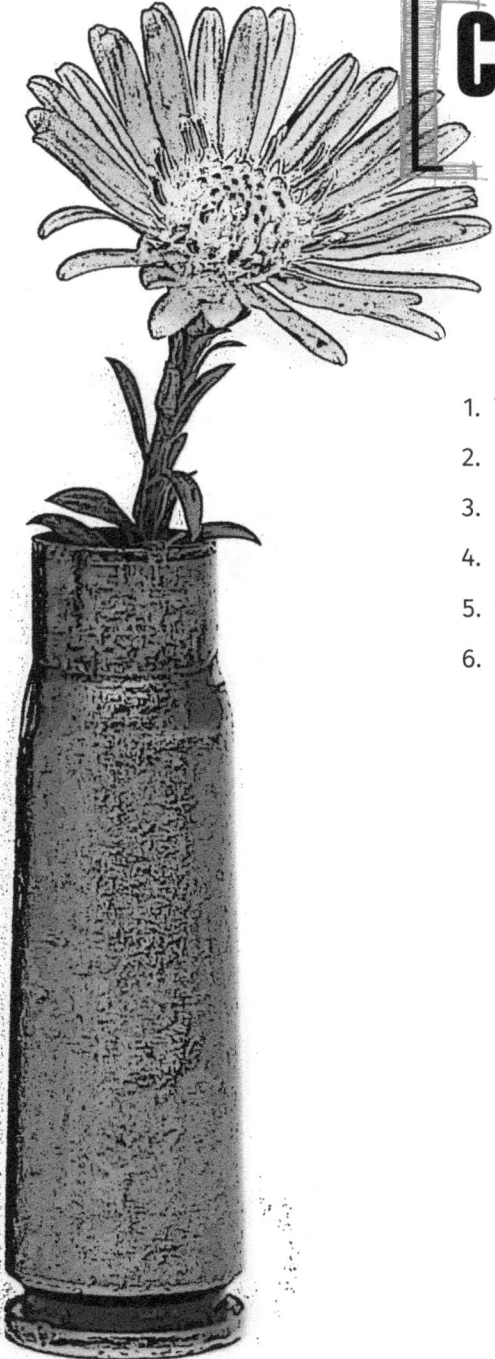

Introduction 5

1. The Roots of Violence. 9

2. Enemies. 15

3. Scapegoats and Sacred Violence . . . 21

4. Sacred Violence No Longer Works . . 29

5. War 37

6. Fear Not. 43

   About the Writer 51

[Introduction]

Violence! We live in the midst of it. News reports highlight it. The United States (my home) was birthed in violence, celebrates violence as entertainment, and spends much of its revenue on the military and weapons. Somehow we know this will not end well.

But how do Jesus' followers live in the midst of violence? Do we:

> Fight it?

> Avoid it?

> Accept it as the way things are?

> Risk our own lives to expose and confront it?

> Organize nonviolent resistence?

> Pray about it?

> Avoid the political process?

> Get involved in the political process?

The six sessions of this Bible study will focus on these questions: How can we avoid getting caught up in the violence around us? How can we be a faithful witness to Jesus, the Word of God, the face of God, the Son of God, the revelation of God's grace and truth?

Siegfried Bartel spoke about how easily German Christians were convinced to support Hitler. A German Mennonite, Bartel served in Hitler's army but later became an outspoken voice for peace. He recalls, "I had accepted [Jesus] as my Lord. I thought I followed him, but I obeyed the State. We had on [our] belt buckles 'God with us' and actually it's a lie. . . . States are misusing Christianity for their purpose."[1]

We, too, are all susceptible to the allure of holy war and sacred violence that promise to defeat evil. My prayer is that this study will provide tools to resist the seduction of war and violence, and strengthen the church's faithful witness.

I approach this study from the perspective of René Girard, who has opened up new ways of understanding Jesus' revelation. Girard was a French literary critic who served as professor in various elite U.S. universities.[2] Girard became a convinced Christian (Catholic) when he discovered in the Gospels an answer to the sacred violence of human sacrifice. Jesus' crucifixion is like countless other murders of innocent victims in the history of sacred violence. The unimaginable difference is that God was revealed in the victim of sacred violence! Never could we humans have imagined that! The victim had always been guilty! The community had always received the gods' approval!

Not so with Jesus. When God raised Jesus from the tomb, the scars of torture and death were still visible on his body. The

1   Amy Dueckman, "Former Soldier Leaves Legacy of Christian Pacifism," *Canadian Mennonite*, February 24, 2016, http://www.canadianmennonite.org/stories/former-soldier-leaves-legacy-christian-pacifism.
2   To learn more about Girard, see René Girard and James G. Williams, ed., *The Girard Reader* (New York: Crossroads Herder, 1996); James Warren, *Compassion or Apocalypse: A Comprehensible Guide to the Thought of René Girard* (Alresford, UK: John Hunt Publishing, 2013); Willard M. Swartley, ed., *Violence Renounced: René Girard, Biblical Studies, and Peacemaking* (Telford, PA: Pandora Press, 2000); Paul Nuechterlein, ed., *Girardian Reflections on the Lectionary*, http://girardianlectionary.net/.

victim had triumphed! God had proclaimed guilty the righteous community and raised the Crucified One to be Lord of all! We are still struggling to understand the imensity of this revelation.

—J. Fred Kauffman

[Pray about It]

Thank you, Jesus our Lord, for your faithful witness to your Abba, the One who sent you! We humans could never have imagined the God of grace and truth that you revealed through your suffering and torture and crucifixion—your victory through death and over death. Thank you. Transform us, Lord, through the power of your Spirit, to be faithful witnesses to you. Amen.

1:
The Roots of Violence

"Grace to you and peace!" Ten of the apostle Paul's letters greet congregations with this blessing.

What we do see is war and violence on the news every day. We read of conflicts or murders in our neighborhoods. Violence is a fact of life in our world, our communities, among our friends, and even in our families. Yet do we see grace and peace in the world around us? What are the roots of this violence? Where is the grace and peace that Paul speaks of? How do we deal with the violence?

Think about these scenarios:

1: Conflict in the nursery—Suzy, a young preschooler, is sitting in the church nursery with toys scattered around her. One toy is near her, though she is only mildly interested in it. Little Sam comes in and surveys the toys. Which one does he want? (Ask any parent!) The one closest to Suzy! As he reaches to take it, Suzy grabs it and clings to it. "I had it first!" "You weren't playing with it!" "Yes, I was! I had it first!" "I wanted it first!" Emotions rise and the toy becomes more and more desirable. Sam's interest in the toy stimulated

Suzy's interest, which sparked the spiraling conflict.
Eventually the toy becomes less important to Suzy than
her fight with Sam, and vice versa.

2: The fall of Adam and Eve—"So when the woman saw that the tree was good for food, and that it was a delight to the eyes, and that the tree was to be desired to make one wise, she took of its fruit and ate; and she also gave some to her husband, who was with her, and he ate" (Genesis 3:6).

3: Work in war-torn Cambodia—My wife and I worked in Cambodia with Mennonite Central Committee (MCC) in the aftermath of the Khmer Rouge revolution and its killing fields. Cambodia then was a political battleground between great powers. We began to realize that there was an unspoken rivalry among foreign aid workers regarding who had the most Cambodian friends in positions of power and who had the latest scoop on the complex political situation. MCC sent us to minister to crying human needs in the name of Christ, but we were tempted to use our Cambodian friends as a means to boost our reputations. Lord, have mercy on us!

René Girard identified a common dynamic in classical literature—
the way one person's desire inflamed the desire of others and led
to conflict. He named this **mimetic desire**, or **mimesis**. It is an
unconscious dynamic where the object of one person's desire is imitated and becomes the focus of desire for others. The focus may be
a precious object such as a toy in the church nursery, or the desire
for honor, affection, recognition, respect, and other aspects.

This concept is demonstrated in Genesis 3, when the tempter stimulated Eve's desire for the fruit by implying that God wanted to
keep the fruit away from her and for himself. It also applies to our
Cambodian relief work, in which personal relationships with politically connected people were the point of unhealthy competition.

We see and experience this deeply human dynamic of mimetic desire from toddlers in preschool to billionaires on Wall Street to powerful countries in conflict. In our world, purse, power, and position, or wealth, power, and fame, are the most common desires that become inflamed. Rivalries for these fill our newspapers and airwaves daily. How many lives are lost every hour as humans vie with each other? How much of our energy do we spend on interpersonal rivalries from unhealthy competition with others?

In his letter, James connects *desire* and *violence*.

> Those conflicts and disputes among you, where do they come from? Do they not come from your cravings [desires] that are at war within you? You want [desire] something and do not have it; so you commit murder. And you covet [desire] something and cannot obtain it; so you engage in disputes and conflicts. You do not have, because you do not ask. You ask and do not receive, because you ask wrongly, in order to spend what you get on your pleasures [desires]. (James 4:1-4)

And remember the disciples' last Passover meal with Jesus? They were caught up in this kind of rivalry for status!

> A dispute also arose among them as to which one of them was to be regarded as the greatest. But he said to them, "The kings of the Gentiles lord it over them; and those in authority over them are called benefactors. But not so with you; rather the greatest among you must become like the youngest, and the leader like one who serves. For who is greater, the one who is at the table or the one who serves? Is it not the one at the table? But I am among you as one who serves." (Luke 22:24-27)

What is the answer to these conflicts? God's grace. "Grace to you and peace." Grace is like gravity—it exists for everyone. We do nothing to create it or deserve it. We don't need to earn it or measure up in order to obtain it. We cannot compete for it nor do anything to get more.

If only we would live by this amazing grace! I wouldn't need to compete with you to prove my worth! God's love is given unconditionally. I wouldn't need to impress my neighbors with my knowledge, or wealth, or influence, because I am a beloved child of God.

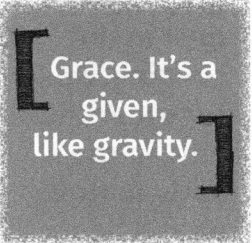

[Grace. It's a given, like gravity.]

[Talk about It]

▶ What examples of mimetic desire do you see around you—in the news, in your community, or even in your family? What are people competing for?

▶ Is there a mimetic rivalry that has you hooked in an unhealthy way? A coworker, a sister or brother in the church, a family member? What is the focus of your rivalry?

▶ Hold that rivalry in mind and consciously open yourself to God's grace. Can that help deflate the rivalry?

[Pray about It]

[For some, this type of prayer happens best in the evening, while for others, it's best in the early morning or at a noon break in the day's activities. Find the most natural time for you.]

▶ Take time to review events and conversations of the past day.

▶ When did you sense God's presence or feel particularly alive? Give thanks.

▶ When did unhealthy rivalries with others claim your energy and attention? Bring this to God in prayer.

▶ Where do you hope to see God at work in your life tomorrow?

2: [Enemies]

OPENING PRAYER

Psalm 139:23-24
Search me, O God, and know my heart;
test me and know my thoughts.
See if there is any wicked way in me,
and lead me in the way everlasting. Amen.

Richard Rohr writes:

We now know from cultural studies and historical experience that groups define themselves and even hold themselves together largely negatively—by who they are not,
what they are against, and what they do not do. We need
a problem or an enemy to gather our energies. We usually
define ourselves through various "purity codes" to sep-
arate ourselves from the "impure" and the presumably
unworthy. Simple worship (what we are for, or in support
of, and what we love) is much harder to sustain.[1]

1   Richard Rohr, "Seven Underlying Themes of Richard Rohr's Teachings:
Fourth Theme," Richard Rohr's Daily Meditation, June 27, 2012,
http://conta.cc/NzPer3.

As Rohr notes, we often define ourselves over against enemies or people we look down on or fear. In fact, the heart of racism is a group that bases its identity on being "better than" others. "I am better than (group)." This says nothing about my own qualities, capabilities, or character; just that I am "better than" the others.

I recall when my sense of superiority as a white man was challenged and shattered. I was shaken by a profound identity crisis. Like many white people in the United States, I based my identity on being unassailably better than those of other races. Take that away, and who was I? Really! Few things are more explosive than

talking about race and identity in the United States because we white people have so deeply internalized that sense of superiority!

In Jesus' day, different Jewish sects had many disagreements, but they all agreed on this: "We are *not* like the Gentiles. We are circumcised. They are uncircumcised." Constant markers were maintained between "us" and "them." In the temple, the wall marking the Court of the Jews had a sign in Greek: "Let no foreigner enter within the parapet and the partition which surrounds the Temple precincts. Anyone caught will be held accountable for his ensuing death."

In American politics today, liberals describe conservatives in degrading and disparaging ways. "How can they be so stupid and prejudiced?" In the meantime, conservatives paint an ugly picture of liberals as immoral baby killers, and as wildly unrealistic. "Do they actually believe that garbage?" These groups define themselves more by who they *aren't* than who they *are*.

> "At the source of hatred of the Other there is hatred of the self." —René Girard

In Jesus' parable of the good Samaritan (Luke 10:25-37), religious leaders—good, moral, upright people—refuse to offer help to a naked, dying man. But the enemy, the other, the impure Samaritan, goes out of his way to help. And Jesus concludes with a command: "Go and do likewise" (v. 37). Not just to help those in need, but to go beyond the notions of "who is your neighbor" to include people who are not liked!

And in another parable, a Pharisee and a tax collector seek God's favor in the temple, but in very different ways.

Two men went up to the temple to pray, one a Pharisee and the other a tax collector.

The Pharisee, standing by himself, was praying thus, "God, I thank you that I am not like other people: thieves, rogues, adulterers, or even like this tax collector. I fast twice a week; I give a tenth of all my income." But the tax collector, standing far off, would not even look up to heaven, but was beating his breast and saying, "God, be merciful to me, a sinner!" I tell you, this man went down to his home justified rather than the other; for all who exalt themselves will be humbled, but all who humble themselves will be exalted. (Luke 18:10-14)

> The Pharisee identified himself by comparing and concluding that he was "not like other people." He exalted himself above others. Meanwhile, the tax collector spoke only of himself and acknowledged that he was a sinner.

In Nazareth when Jesus preached his first sermon in his home synagogue (Luke 4), he dared to suggest that God worked through Naaman the Syrian and the widow of Zarephath. They were foreigners! They were not Jews! They were the enemy! Jesus' teaching enraged the neighbors. They tried to kill him. In their world, the Jews were God's (good) people, and the Gentiles were vile, unclean enemies of God. When Jesus suggested that God also chose Gentiles, he attacked the center of their identity.

[Talk about It]

▶ Summarize Jesus' teaching in the three Scripture texts mentioned in this session. What was he getting at?

▶ As a nation today, what do we contrast ourselves with to create our national identity? (A few decades ago in the United States, it was communism.)

▶ Reflect on the roots of the European sense of superiority. It runs very deep. For centuries, Europeans have given themselves exalted status, often claiming Christian heritage and "having the truth" as the reason. And from that claim of superiority has flowed the colonization of nations around the globe, with massive bloodshed and the destruction of ancient local cultures. It also justified slavery in the United States. (Lord, have mercy!) Learn more about the Doctrine of Discovery and efforts to dismantle it at http://dofdmenno.org.

▶ In your community (church or neighborhood), who are the people who are looked down on? Feared? How has this affected your sense of self?

[Pray about It]

▶ Each day, pray this prayer adapted from Psalm 131:

O LORD, may my heart not be proud, may my eyes not look down on others.

May I not occupy myself with things too great and too marvelous for me.

Help me, Lord, to calm and quiet my soul in silence and peace.

Like a child at rest in its mother's arms,

may my soul be within me.

And may we, your people, put our hope in you from this time on and forevermore.

[3: Scapegoats and Sacred Violence]

OPENING PRAYER

Psalm 139:23-24
Search me, O God, and know my heart;
test me and know my thoughts.
See if there is any wicked way in me,
and lead me in the way everlasting. Amen.

"Scapegoat!" Ever wonder where this term comes from? It's from an actual goat!

Leviticus 16 describes preparations for the Day of Atonement. During the ritual, two goats are brought to Aaron. He casts lots to see which will be offered as a burnt offering to the Lord and which one is to be sent away to the wilderness for Azazel.

> Then Aaron shall lay both his hands on the head of the live goat, and confess over it all the iniquities of the people of Israel, and all their transgressions, all their sins, putting them on the head of the goat, and sending it away into the

wilderness by means of someone designated for the task. The goat shall bear on itself all their iniquities to a barren region. (Leviticus 16:21-22)

> The goat is chosen by lot, through random choice or divine will?

> All the sins of the community are laid upon it.

> It is expelled from the community.

Today, people have identified cyberbullying as a means of scapegoating. Phoebe Prince committed suicide in 2009 as a result of cyberbullying at high school. She and her mother had moved to the United States from a small town in Ireland, and she enrolled in the ninth grade. She developed friendships with two older boys who had girlfriends. The girls claimed that Phoebe was not playing by the rules.

> That dynamic can happen with a person or group, too, when
>> > they are chosen randomly as the "scapegoat";
>> > all the problems of a community are blamed on them; and
>> > they are ostracized.

The girls began to berate Phoebe and on social media posted mean taunts, calling her an "Irish slut." Others who had no relationship with the boys or their girlfriends joined in the cyberbullying. The shaming was relentless. In January 2010, Phoebe hung herself at home.[1]

In U.S. history, scapegoating happened with the lynching of African Americans. A 1940 research project examined cotton prices between 1882 and 1930 and lynchings in the Deep South. As cotton prices dropped, the number of lynchings went up. White people became angry and frustrated when cotton prices were low, and black men became the scapegoats even though they had nothing to do with the price of cotton.[2]

I have a haunting memory from my time as a dormitory manager. At an open house for potential students, I met a young African American man considering the college. Later that day, someone set off a cherry bomb in the dorm's stairwell just as a student was going up the steps. As a result, the student had serious ear pain. A few people gathered there, discussing what

---

1   James O'Higgins Norman and Justin Connolly, "Mimetic Theory and Scapegoating in the Age of Cyberbullying: The Case of Phoebe Prince," *Pastoral Care in Education*, November 22, 2011.
2   Steven J. Breckler, James Olson, and Elizabeth Wiggins, *Social Psychology Alive* (Belmont CA: Thompson Learning, 2006), 359.

happened. The young African American man joined the conversation. Someone asked, "Who would do this?" I looked around the group, wondering the same thing. When I looked at the African American, I saw a look of terror in his eyes. He said, "Oh, no!" He turned and hurried away. I never saw him again.

What did he see in my eyes? An accusatory look? I still shudder at the thought! He sensed danger. He knew instinctively how crowds can turn on someone. He felt threatened even though he had nothing to do with the cherry bomb. I think he knew in his bones about the scapegoating mechanism!

René Girard recreates a typical scene—members of a primitive community have fallen into intense rivalry. The rivalries are boiling up and threaten to destroy the whole community. People are full of high anxiety. Suddenly one person, who is different in some way, catches the group's attention. And in a rush of agreement, everyone agrees that the one who is different is causing the threat.

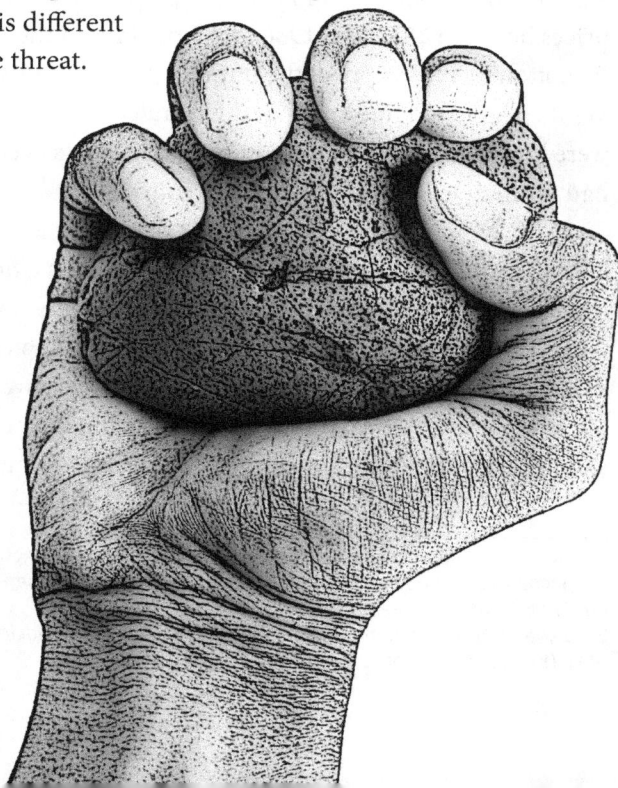

All the anger and fear of the community are poured onto the one who is different, and the group rushes together to stone the victim. As the victim lies dead and bleeding, the group experience something powerful and mysterious! Harmony has been restored. The tension is gone!

The community is mystified. A transformation happened when the victim's blood was shed! That must mean that

> the victim really was evil; and

> the gods are pleased with the sacrifice.

Eventually another round of conflict would be contained with another victim; and often this would become a sacred ritual.

Girard believes that the cathartic experience of killing the scapegoat was, in fact, the foundation of primitive religions and cultures.

Human sacrifice to the gods was common in many cultures of the world,[3] including among my Germanic ancestors. At the time of the New Testament, they were offering human sacrifices as part of their traditional religion. They had created a sacred ritual out of their primitive experience of killing scapegoats. Publius Tacitus, a first-century Roman senator and historian, observed that German tribes practiced human sacrifice, not in temples, but "in a grove hallowed by auguries of the fathers."[4] They continued this practice until the growth of Christian faith among them in the fifth century.

---

3   Mike Parker-Pearson, "The Practice of Human Sacrifice," BBC, last modified February 28, 2011, http://www.bbc.co.uk/history/ancient/british_prehistory/human_sacrifice_01.shtml.
4   Cornelius Tacitus, "Germania," Our Civilization, March 22, 2017, http://www.ourcivilisation.com/smartboard/shop/tacitusc/germany/chap1.htm.

J SCHNORR VON CAROLSFELD

In John's account of the woman found in adultery (John 8:1-11), the real intent of her accusers was not to seek justice according to the law. If so, where was the man caught in the act of adultery? Instead, the crowd was upset by the way Jesus was destabilizing and threatening their "clean" community. They were eager to unleash a communal "cleansing" by stoning this sinner, and to implicate Jesus in the process.

> The scribes and the Pharisees brought a woman who had been caught in adultery; and making her stand before all of them, they said to him, "Teacher, this woman was caught in the very act of committing adultery. Now in the law Moses commanded us to stone such women. Now what do you say?" They said this to test him, so that they might have some charge to bring against him. Jesus bent down and

wrote with his finger on the ground. When they kept on
questioning him, he straightened up and said to them, "Let
anyone among you who is without sin be the first to throw
a stone at her." And once again he bent down and wrote on
the ground. When they heard it, they went away, one by one,
beginning with the elders; and Jesus was left alone with the
woman standing before him. Jesus straightened up and said
to her, "Woman, where are they? Has no one condemned
you?" She said, "No one, sir." And Jesus said, "Neither do
I condemn you. Go your way, and from now on do not sin
again." (John 8:3-11)

The religious leaders were seeking a cleansing of community guilt and sin by stoning a woman they believed was sinful.
This cleansing would require no effort on the crowd's part to
deal with their inner faults. Jesus challenged them to look within
themselves first, and refused to support their use of scapegoating
to make themselves feel righteous.

During his last week in Jerusalem, Jesus created tensions. The
Roman military was on high alert, and the chief priest knew that
he was on a powder keg.

The chief priests and the Pharisees called a meeting of the
council, and said, "What are we to do? This man is perform-
ing many signs. If we let him go on like this, everyone will
believe in him, and the Romans will come and destroy both
our holy place and our nation." But one of them, Caiaphas,
who was high priest that year, said to them, "You know nothing at all! You do not understand that it is better for you to
have one man die for the people than to have the whole nation destroyed." (John 11:47-50)

[Talk about It]

▶ Discuss the experience of Jesus described in John 11. What was happening?

▶ Have you witnessed a crowd turn on a victim—either in your experience or in a news report? Have you ever been the scapegoat?

▶ What person or group do you think is being scapegoated to-day? What are they blamed for? What is the real problem that the community or society is facing?

▶ What do you think of Girard's theory that primitive humans shaped their religious beliefs out of the experience of sacred violence against a scapegoat victim?

[Pray about It]

▶ Explore and share with Jesus your thoughts and feelings about his experience of being the scapegoat, and what it cost him.

▶ Ask for clarity to see persons or groups being scapegoated today.

▶ Seek God's guidance about how to respond.

4: Sacred Violence No Longer Works

OPENING PRAYER

Psalm 139:23-24
Search me, O God, and know my heart;
test me and know my thoughts.
See if there is any wicked way in me,
and lead me in the way everlasting. Amen.

"You would get a far better understanding of the National Rifle Association if you were approaching us as one of the great religions of the world." So said the then NRA executive vice president J. Warren Cassidy in a 2001 interview with *Time* magazine.[1] The NRA may be a pagan religion, but it has nothing to do with the revelation of God in Jesus, the triumphant victim, who rose from the dead with the marks of his execution still visible.

---

1 Richard Lacayo, "Under Fire," *Time*, June 24, 2001, http://content.time.com/time/magazine/article/0,9171,153695,00.html.

Evangelical pastor Rob Schenk, president of the Washington, D.C.—based Faith and Action ministry, writes:

> I believe the increased presence of firearms among American evangelicals, including pastors that are now armed in the pulpit and ready to shoot into the congregation if necessary, signals a serious moral crisis in the church. Those who should be all about the good news of God's saving love for humanity are instead being led astray by a popular gun culture that contradicts the teaching and model of

> In Gethsemane, Jesus told Peter to put his sword away, saying, "For all who take the sword will perish by the sword" (Matthew 26:52).

Jesus. . . . This pro-gun enthusiasm presents us with a temptation to abandon our faith in the one true God and trade it for a neo-pagan, fear-driven, earth-bound religion.[2]

In 2013, Philadelphia council member Kenyatta Johnson organized a public vigil to lament two recent shooting deaths. I joined in, marching and chanting, "Stop the violence!" At each street corner, people paused to speak out. "Put down the guns!" neighbors pleaded. "We're killing ourselves!"

I was the only white person there, and I felt uncomfortable, as though I was watching a private family fight, a conversation meant to be internal. Testimonies of loss and grief seemed to pose the questions, "What is wrong with us? Why are we doing this?"

When the council member asked me to close in prayer, I noted, "I hear you speak of your commitment to deal with violence in your community. I wish you well. But I want you to know that the local gun shop owners look like me (white). They resist our requests that they avoid selling multiple guns to people who will flip them illegally onto the streets. And it is men that look like me in our state legislature who block effective laws to control illegal gun trafficking. I cannot begin to understand the violence that you face, but I am committed to working with my people, especially white Christians, to find ways to stop the flood of illegal guns that are feeding the violence here."

---

2   Rob Schenck, "Should Christians Own Guns?" *Sojourners*, May 2016.

Mr. Johnson put his arm around me and said, "This is another dimension of our problem. We need ways to stop the illegal trafficking of handguns!" In 2012, Philadelphia had over 280 gun deaths,[3] and in every case the murder weapon had been illegally trafficked. By comparison, there were 172 gun deaths in all of Canada that year.[4]

Gun homicides per 100,000 residents

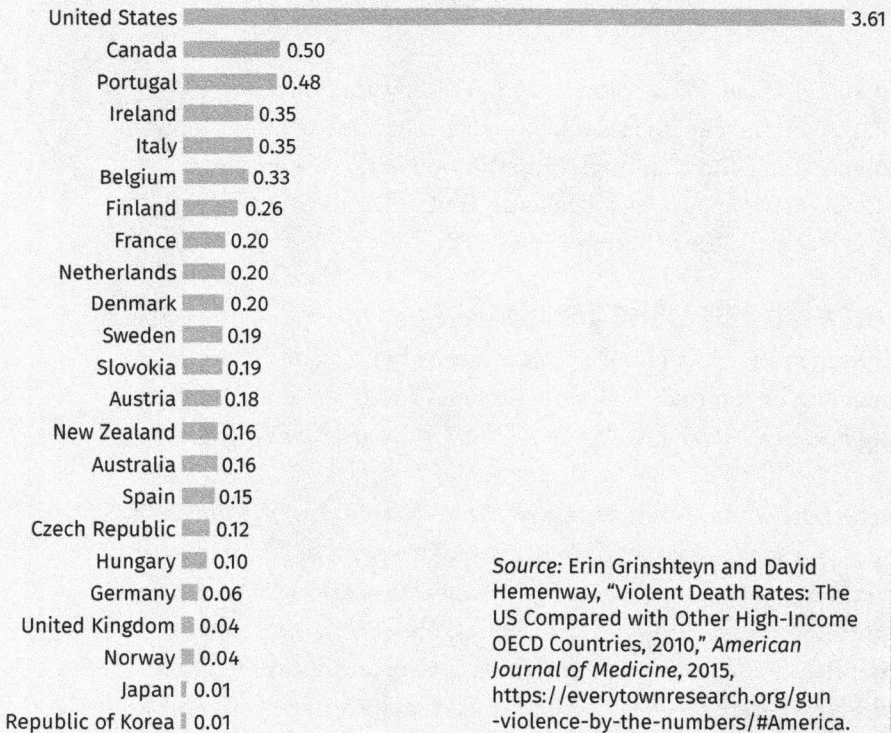

United States	3.61
Canada	0.50
Portugal	0.48
Ireland	0.35
Italy	0.35
Belgium	0.33
Finland	0.26
France	0.20
Netherlands	0.20
Denmark	0.20
Sweden	0.19
Slovokia	0.19
Austria	0.18
New Zealand	0.16
Australia	0.16
Spain	0.15
Czech Republic	0.12
Hungary	0.10
Germany	0.06
United Kingdom	0.04
Norway	0.04
Japan	0.01
Republic of Korea	0.01

Source: Erin Grinshteyn and David Hemenway, "Violent Death Rates: The US Compared with Other High-Income OECD Countries, 2010," *American Journal of Medicine*, 2015, https://everytownresearch.org/gun-violence-by-the-numbers/#America.

3   Research and Planning Unit, Philadelphia Police Department, "Murder/Shooting Analysis 2012," March 21, 2013, https://www.phillypolice.com/assets/crime-maps-stats/PPD-Homicide-Analysis-2011-vs-2012.pdf.
4   Fram Dinshaw, "How American Gun Deaths and Gun Laws Compare to Canada's," *National Observer*, December 24, 2015, http://www.nationalobserver.com/2015/12/04/news/how-american-gun-deaths-and-gun-laws-compare-canadas.

In the previous three sessions of this study, we studied Girard's theory of mimetic desire and rivalry, and the way that communities have controlled the spread of violence through scapegoating and human sacrifice.

This primitive sacred violence used to have tremendous power! It used to preserve communities by turning all-against-all violence to all-against-one. By killing a scapegoat, communities could blow off violent energy in a channeled way to restore harmony. The way this worked was stunning and mystifying, the earliest experience of the sacred—both frightening and beneficial!

People created myths to explain why the gods rewarded sacrifice. They developed taboos and prohibitions around what was sacred and what was profane. Tying it all together was the practice of human sacrifice, the power of the lynch mob. It all depended, however, on everyone agreeing that the *victim* really was guilty and that the gods wanted the sacrifice.

[**Jesus smashed these sacred myths!**]

The account of Jesus' death is not really unusual. He upset the rulers of a community. They came together against him (even Pilate and Herod, who were enemies). They accused him of breaking a sacred code (blasphemy). They stirred up the crowd to call for his death. And they killed him, certain that they were righteous and doing God's will. **This is typical scapegoating violence!**

[**So what makes Jesus' case different?**]

Jesus, the tortured and crucified *victim*, turned out to be the just and righteous one, and the religious community had united to have him murdered! Jesus, the *victim*, rose from the dead, triumphant, but with the marks of his murder still visible on his hands, feet, and side. This was utterly unthinkable!

> **No one could have imagined this! It took a revelation!**

Since that earthquake revelation, the world has been
more and more aware of the perspectives and experiences of the victims of human violence. The myths of sacred violence have been broken. God was revealed in a murdered victim!

Girard notes that wherever the gospel takes root, blood sacrifices disappear forever. But that very "blood sacrifice" was what was used to keep violence from spreading and destroying the whole community. So when sacrifice no longer works, rivalries are free to flourish and multiply, and violence begets more violence. "For all who take the sword will perish by the sword" (Matthew 26:52). How do the "chief priests" of America's gun culture and religion respond to high-profile gun violence? They say, "We need more guns!"

[Talk about It]

▶ Guns for self-protection?

> The University of Pennsylvania did research on assaults between 2003 and 2006 in Philadelphia. They found that people carrying a gun during an assault were four and a half times more likely to be shot than those who had no gun.[5]

> The FBI tracks "justifiable" homicides: "The killing of a felon, during the commission of a felony, by a private citizen." In 2015 there were 268 cases of "justifiable homicide" by gun, 0.9% of average annual gun deaths. There were 9,587 gun murders and 21,334 gun suicides that year.[6]

▶ I recently spoke with an older white Christian from the suburbs about my concerns with the gun culture. He responded, "I'm part of the gun culture! I have 18 guns." "So you're a collector, right?" I asked. "No!" he said, "they are for my own protection." Do you think he feels safe with his 18 guns?

▶ Has gun violence touched your life? If so, how?

5   Charles Branas et al., "Investigating the Link between Gun Possession and Gun Assault," *American Journal of Public Health* 99, no. 11 (November 2009): 2034–2040, https://www.ncbi.nlm.nih.gov/pmc/articles/PMC2759797/.
6   U.S. Department of Justice, "Crime in the United States, 2015," September 26, 2016, https://ucr.fbi.gov/crime-in-the-u.s/2015/crime-in-the-u.s.-2015/resource-pages/2015-cius-summary_final.pdf.

▶ Jesus broke the power of primitive sacred religious violence that used to keep violence from spreading out of control. How can Jesus' followers live in his revelation and bear witness to his rejection of violence?

[Pray about It]

▶ Lift up to Jesus incidents of violence producing more violence in our world today. Pray that Jesus' followers would find ways to bear witness to another way. Give thanks for evidence of that witness in your own life or in the lives of others.

ZEN/THINKSTOCK

5: [War]

OPENING PRAYER

Psalm 139:23-24
Search me, O God, and know my heart;
test me and know my thoughts.
See if there is any wicked way in me,
and lead me in the way everlasting.
Amen.

Nations often describe their war as a godly fight against evil. United States President George W. Bush spoke at the White House on September 16, 2001, and said, "My administration has a job to do and we're going to do it. We will rid the world of the evildoers."[1]

---

1 Manuel Perez-Rivas, "Bush Vows to Rid the World of 'Evil-Doers,'" CNN, September 16, 2001, http://edition.cnn.com/2001/US/09/16/gen.bush.terrorism/.

Osama bin Laden wrote in his letter to the American people, "The Islamic Nation . . . was able to dismiss and destroy the previous evil Empires like yourself; the [Islamic] Nation . . . rejects your attacks, wishes to remove your evils, and is prepared to fight you."[2]

This is not the language of foreign policy analysis—**it is religious language!**

> **The religious myth of war is far removed from the experience of actual warriors.**

In 2016 I joined my wife to visit her home country, Vietnam, for one of her work trips. After I returned to my home in Philadelphia, I talked with a friend who had served with the

---

2 "Bin Laden's 'Letter to America,'" *Guardian*, November 24, 2002, https://www.theguardian.com/world/2002/nov/24/theobserver.

Marines in Vietnam. I encouraged him to go see the country again. "I'll *never* go back to that country!" he exclaimed. "Not after what I did there." Fifty years later, what haunts him is "what I did."

Former U.S. senator Bob Kerrey won a Medal of Honor in Vietnam. He once led a combat mission behind enemy lines. They came to a clearing with thatched huts and opened fire. In an interview with the *New York Times*, he said, "The thing I will remember until the day I die is walking in and finding, I don't know, 14 or so . . . women and children who were dead."[3] He said in another interview, "I'm tired of people describing me as a hero and **holding this inside**."[4]

Philip Jones Griffiths, a Vietnam War photojournalist, said, "In Washington there is a memorial to the U.S. deaths in the Vietnam War and it is 150 yards long. If the same memorial was built for the Vietnamese that were killed it would be **9 miles long**."[5]

In his book *War Is a Force That Gives Us Meaning*, Chris Hedges reflects on 20 years of reporting from the front lines of wars. He writes:

I have been in ambushes on desolate stretches of Central American roads, shot at in the marshes of southern Iraq, imprisoned in the Sudan, beaten by Saudi military police, deported from Libya and Iran, . . . held for a week by the Iraqi Republican Guard . . . strafed by Russian Mig-21s in Bosnia, fired upon by Serb snipers, and shelled for days in Sarajevo with deafening rounds of heavy artillery. . . . I have seen too much of violent death. . . . War exposes the capacity for evil

3   Gregory L. Vistica, "What Happened in Thanh Phong," *New York Times Magazine*, April 29, 2001, 51.
4   Dennis Farney, "Former Senator Bob Kerrey Discloses His Wartime in Role in Civilian Killings," *Wall Street Journal*, April 25, 2001, A22.
5   Quoted in "Veterans for Peace Annual Spring Tour to Viet Nam 2017," Veterans for Peace, October 21, 2016, https://www.veteransforpeace.org/who-we-are/member-highlights/2016/10/21/veterans-peace-annual-spring-tour-viet-nam-2017.

that lurks not far below the surface within all of us. . . . [But] the enduring attraction of war is this: Even with its destruction and carnage it can give us what we long for in life. It can give us purpose, meaning, a reason for living. Only when we are in the midst of conflict does the shallowness and vapidness of much of our lives become apparent. Trivia dominates our conversations and increasingly our airwaves. And war is an enticing elixir. It gives us resolve, a cause. It allows us to be noble.[6]

Hedges has an MDiv from Harvard University and remains rooted in the stories and experience of faith. He is not a pacifist, though he has seen so much bloodshed that he reacts viscerally to the myths that propel nations to wage war.

> Nothing ignites the human heart like going to war to kill God's enemies. It puts us on God's elite team and gives our killing a sacred purpose.

I believe that in our day, **the idea of holy war** and fighting evil has taken the place of ritualized human sacrifice. War deflects a nation's problems onto an evil other, and unites splintered societies. But those sent into battle pay a steep price.

On newscasts we witness the physical destruction of war—cities leveled, homes destroyed, bodies blown to bits. But we do not see the devastation that survivors live with—both the perpetrators and the victims. We do not see young people placed in hellish situations as soldiers who end up doing things that haunt them the rest of their lives. **Moral injury**, it has been called.

---

6   Chris Hedges, *War Is a Force That Gives Us Meaning* (New York: Anchor, 2003), 2–3.

As I was writing this chapter, I heard the news that an Iraq war veteran had killed five people in the Fort Lauderdale, Florida, airport. The shooter's aunt told a reporter that her nephew talked about the destruction he witnessed during the war, about the killing of children. "His mind was not right," she said. He had asked authorities for help, according to his brother, but did not get the treatment he needed. *Moral injury.*

[Talk about It]

▶ The Peace and Justice Support Network of Mennonite Church USA has a study regarding challenges that returning veterans face. It states: "Moral Injury, a type of wounding of the soul or conscience, can stay with a veteran long after their military service concludes. . . . [It includes] feelings of shame, regret and fear."[7]

▶ Eastern Mennonite University's Center for Justice and Peacebuilding (Harrisonburg, Va.) trains people to walk with veterans through the moral injury that they may have experienced. For more information, look up the workshop "The Journey Home from War" (http://www.emu.edu/cjp/star/ training/the-journey-home-from-war/). Another site that provides good information is the veteran's ministry of St. Andrews Church of the United Church of Christ (http://www .standrewsucc.org/veterans-ministry-team-touchstone-veterans -outreach).

> Are there people in your church who are willing to prepare themselves to respond with compassion to war veterans whose hearts and souls have been wounded?

7 "Returning Veterans," Peace and Justice Support Network, accessed March 25, 2017, http://www.pjsn.org/vets/Pages/default.aspx.

▶ How do Jesus' words speak to us in today's political context? Are we willing to stand before "governors and kings" to be a witness to Jesus (see Mark 13:7-13)? How can we raise our voices against wars and rumors of wars?

> When you hear of wars and rumors of wars, do not be alarmed; this must take place, but the end is still to come. For nation will rise against nation, and kingdom against kingdom; . . . you will stand before governors and kings because of me, as a testimony to them. . . . And you will be hated by all because of my name. But the one who endures to the end will be saved. (Mark 13:7-13)

[Pray about It]

▶ Lift up to Jesus those places in the world currently experiencing war. Ask that Jesus' followers in those places, and around them, can find ways to bear witness to peace that is not like the world's peace.

6:

[Fear Not]

Psalm 139:23-24
Search me, O God, and know my heart;
test me and know my thoughts.
See if there is any wicked way in me,
and lead me in the way everlasting. Amen.

In his book *Choosing against War: A Christian View*, John D. Roth writes:

How might Christians look on the world differently, if we actually—literally—believed that God's love was indeed stronger than our fears? What would happen if we assumed that our allegiance to God, our identity with Christ and our commitment to the church would call us to respond to the world's pain differently than our non-Christian neighbors? In the face

[**"We create our enemy in the image of our fears."**
—Anonymous]

of violence, are there any options open to the Christian believer other than the default impulse toward patriotic unity and a steely determination to exact "an eye for an eye"?[1]

"There's a war going on today! And if you don't know it, you are going to lose the battle!" says chaplain Ronald Muse, a man I know in Philadelphia. A hardheaded former gang member, Muse was rescued from a life of drugs and violence by a Damascus Road–type encounter with Jesus on a street corner. Ronald lost none of his grit and determination, but now he brings

> **"Do not be afraid!"** occurs 62 times in the New Revised Standard Version **of the Bible. "Do not fear!"** appears 44 times.

1   John D. Roth, *Choosing against War: A Christian View* (Intercourse, PA: Good Books, 2002), 8.

those transformed gifts to his ministry in the city's prisons. He speaks with the intensity of a soldier in a firefight. This is not a game. It's life. It's real. And he is determined to open people's hearts and minds to the transformation that is possible, and to the possibility of victory in battle.

"There's a war going on, but the first place you need to focus is in your own life!" he teaches. "That's where the war starts! You have to have your inner image transformed. If Christ changes your inner image, your behavior will change. I have heard so many sermons about how 'those people' need the gospel. Forget it! *You* need the gospel. *I* need the gospel. It has to do its work within us first!"

Chaplain Muse does not engage in the war raging around him with the weapons of street violence, or of the police. But he walks into the middle of the conflict without fear, into the Philadelphia prisons, equipped, as he says, "with the whole armor of God." He finds Ephesians 6:11-17 to be a continual source of encouragement and strength.

In Paul's "whole armor of God" imagery, he acknowledges that there is a war going on, and that Jesus' people need to take it seriously. But the weapons he describes are not offensive weapons to be used in an attack. They are defensive, to protect from the evil one's attacks—truth, righteousness or justice (same word in Greek), peace, faith, salvation, and the sword (a small defensive dagger), which is the Word of God.

In Revelation, John describes world-shattering violence with wars, beasts, and dragons. But John does not urge Jesus' followers to join the fray. He calls them, instead, to patient endurance in faithfulness

to Jesus, the Lamb that was slain.[2] That may sound tame, but look at the trouble it brought John, exiled from his home because of the Word of God and the testimony of Jesus.

How do we live in the midst of a violent world without being drawn into its violence? How do we resist its seduction and bear witness to the way of Jesus and the kingdom that he proclaimed? How can we, like Ronald Muse, walk into the battle equipped with the whole armor of God to bear witness to another way?

There are three suggestions.

1. Do not fear.

Take seriously this repeated command in Scripture; "For God did not give us a spirit of cowardice [or fear], but rather a spirit of power and of love and of self-discipline" (2 Timothy 1:7). Resist attempts by political leaders to play on people's fears. Resist the creation of a *scapegoat* enemy.

2. Get to know the enemy.

Seek out people demonized as "the enemy." Learn to know them. Build a relationship with them. Share meals with them. Chris Hedges shares a beautiful example of this:

> During the Balkan war a Serbian Christian couple was trapped in their home by intense shelling. They were surrounded by Bosnian Muslims, and their infant daughter was near starvation when someone knocked on their door. It was a Muslim farmer, and he handed them a half liter of milk. He came every day for over a year. Muslim neighbors became angry, telling him to give milk to Muslim babies and let the Christians starve. He did not answer them, and he never accepted payment.[3]

---

2 See Revelation 1:9; 2:2-3.
3 Hedges, *War Is a Force*, 50–51.

3. Imitate Jesus.

According to René Girard, "The imitation of Christ protects us from mimetic rivalries. . . . No existence is free from imitation, and the alternative to imitating Christ or Christ-like models is the imitation of our neighbors."[4]

The apostle Paul invites us to imitate Christ:

Let the same mind be in you that was in Christ Jesus

> who, though he was in the form of God,
>   did not regard equality with God
>   as something to be exploited,
> but emptied himself,
>   taking the form of a slave,
>   being born in human likeness.
> And being found in human form,
>   he humbled himself
>   and became obedient to the point of death—
>   even death on a cross. (Philippians 2:5-8)

---

4   René Girard, "Violence Renounced: Response by René Girard," in *Violence Renounced*, ed. Willard M. Swartley, 310–11.

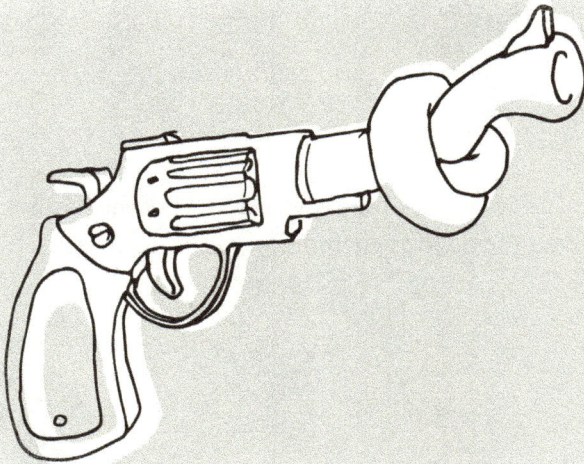

[Talk about It]

▶ There are wars going on! Where do you see battles being fought? Take time as a group to list the battles you see. (International? National? Local community? Church? Family?) Who is at war? What are the fears behind the war? Who are the enemies? What are they fighting over?

▶ Read Psalm 139. The psalmist describes God's care, and praises God's wisdom, when all of a sudden he bursts out with rage:

> O that you would kill the wicked, O God,
>   and that the bloodthirsty would depart from me—
> those who speak of you maliciously,
>   and lift themselves up against you for evil!
> Do I not hate those who hate you, O Lord?
>   And do I not loathe those who rise up against you?
> I hate them with perfect hatred;
>   I count them my enemies. (Psalm 139:19-22)

> What triggered this outrage?

> We don't know who the enemies are, but the psalmist considered them God's enemies as well as his own.

> Then suddenly, the psalmist turns back to check his own heart—as though he caught himself—and in a contrite spirit he prays:

> Search me, O God, and know my heart;
>   test me and know my thoughts.
> See if there is any wicked way in me [not my enemies?],
>   and lead me in the way everlasting.
> (Psalm 139:23-24)

[Pray about It]

▶ Name some people or groups that makes you the most angry. Acknowledge the reality of the harm that they could do. Acknowledge the depth of feeling that you have.

▶ Pray as the psalmist did:

> Search me, O God, and know my heart;
>   test me and know my thoughts.
> See if there is any wicked way in me,
>   and lead me in the way everlasting. Amen.

[About the Writer]

J. Fred Kauffman grew up in Beemer (Neb.) Mennonite Church with two brothers. (Where he first learned about mimetic rivalries!) He attended Hesston (Kans.) College, served two years with Mennonite Voluntary Service in Puerto Rico, and graduated from Goshen (Ind.) College in 1973 with a degree in Spanish.

At college he met international student Nguyen Thi Minh from Vietnam, and they were married in Saigon in 1973. Minh and Fred served with Mennonite Central Committee (MCC) in Guatemala, India, and Cambodia. They lived in Thailand while working for a Baptist development group.

Fred has served as pastor at West Philadelphia Mennonite Fellowship and Methacton Mennonite Church. He worked as MCC's Philadelphia program coordinator, enjoyed building relationships among congregations in the Kingdom Builders Anabaptist Network of Greater Philadelphia, and was on the planning committee for the conference "Heeding God's Call: A Gathering on Peace." He serves on the board of the Crossroads Community Center.

Fred and Minh have two adult sons. Fred enjoys following the Philadelphia Phillies, playing guitar and mandolin, doing woodworking, and being a contented old oddball.

www.ingramcontent.com/pod-product-compliance
Lightning Source LLC
Chambersburg PA
CBHW031634040426
42452CB00007B/825